Private Labeling Bible

Everything You Need To Know, Step-By-Step, To Build a Six-Figure Passive Income

Michael Moosly

Table of contents

Introduction

I want to thank you and congratulate you for purchasing the book, "Amazon FBA: Private Labeling Bible: Everything You Need to Know, Step-By-Step, To Build a Six-Figure Passive Income." This book contains proven steps and strategies for building your own line of products to be sold through Amazon's Marketplace using its Fulfillment by Amazon service as a third-party seller.

In 2015 Amazon became the fastest company in history to reach $100 billion in annual sales. Meanwhile, 50% of all units sold on Amazon were sold by third-party sellers. Of these third-party sellers, over 70,000 were able to achieve annual revenue of over $100,000 (2015)[1].

After reading this book, you will have a solid understanding of each of the stages necessary in developing your

---

[1] 2015 Amazon.com Letter to Shareholders

own private label business on Amazon. These essential stages are the "mechanical" aspects of building a private label business using FBA and represent such topics as "which sites to sign up for," "how to find suppliers," "where to ship your products," "how to obtain reviews," and more. No FBA-based business can function without solid mechanics.

Although a solid understanding of "mechanics" is an absolute basic requirement, what will truly set your business apart is your ability to grasp market dynamics (consumer demand and existing supply) and to locate and build successful relationships with suppliers -- the "art" side of the business. Success is built through offering excellent products at the right price. This book will go beyond mechanics by offering proven strategies for building the skill set to locate and evaluate potential products, find the best suppliers, and optimize your listing according to Amazon's key search engine metrics

Many of the resources readily available on the web focus on "retail-arbitrage" -- in other words finding a product cheaper in one place and selling it in another for a higher price. While this method can certainly be an effective way to provide a modest-to-medium-sized side income or allow a new seller who is low on startup capital to break into FBA, it is not capable of providing large-scale passive income. This book will focus on the private labeling approach, which requires more market research and more "mechanical" work up front, but in return offers the potential to make $100k or more in passive income.

If some of this jargon leaves you feeling intimidated, please don't be. Clear cut definitions and processes linkages will be presented along the way to build your understanding of how the most important elements fit together. You do not need to be a web wizard, programmer, or anything like that to succeed in private labeling. You simply need a drive to understand products and how people shop on Amazon (and in general).

The structure of the book will be as follows:

First, FBA will be defined. Next, a broad example of an entire hypothetical private labelling product venture will be discussed. The aim of doing this early in the book is to demystify the process and give you a framework for understanding where in the overall FBA process each of the topics discussed in subsequent chapters fits. From here, the critical topics of product evaluation, finding suppliers, and Amazon search engine optimization will be explained in greater detail. The final chapters of the book will include discussions of useful tools and utilities, great resources for further reading, and legal structure of your business.

Thanks again for purchasing this book, I hope you enjoy it!

This document is geared towards providing exact and reliable information in regards to the topic and issue covered. The publication is sold with the idea that the publisher is not required to render accounting, officially permitted, or otherwise, qualified services. If advice is necessary, legal or professional, a practiced individual in the profession should be ordered.

- From a Declaration of Principles which was accepted and approved equally by a Committee of the American Bar Association and a Committee of Publishers and Associations.

The information provided herein is stated to be truthful and consistent, in that any liability, in terms of inattention or otherwise, by any usage or abuse of any policies, processes, or directions contained within is the solitary and utter responsibility of the recipient reader. Under no circumstances will any legal responsibility or blame be held against the publisher for any

Chapter 1 – What is FBA?

Chances are, if you are reading this book, you probably have some degree of exposure to Amazon.com, even if it's just as a consumer. Perhaps you've even invested in being an Amazon Prime member in order to take advantage of free two day shipping on the millions of products available through Prime. In deciding whether or not to pay the annual flat fee of $100 to be a member of Prime, a customer must make an estimate of whether his or her total shipping charges for the year's worth of purchases on Amazon will exceed the fee. If so, it makes sense to sign up for prime.   In his 2015 letter to shareholders, CEO Jeff Bezos explained that his goal was to make the purchase of an Amazon Prime membership so advantageous to the consumer that he or she would be irresponsible to not buy it. As mentioned, in 2015, the number of items for sale on Prime increased from 1 million to 30 million.

It's safe to say Bezos is succeeding in his mission to incentivize consumers to purchase a prime membership. But that accomplishment begs the question of how such a dramatic increase was possible? This increase is mostly attributable to the Fulfillment by Amazon (FBA) program and how it enables third-party sellers to utilize Amazon's website to list their own products and make use of Amazon's swift and efficient distribution network to sell their items as "Prime" with free two day shipping. Sellers accomplish this by listing their merchandise on Amazon's Marketplace and then sending their merchandise directly to Amazon to be stocked in one of their many warehouses. Each time a purchase is made, it's more or less "out of sight, 0ut of mind" for the seller, as Amazon ships the unit directly to the purchaser via free two day shipping (assuming the buyer is a Prime member) and automatically adjusts the inventory of the seller. Likewise, Amazon will also process customer returns through its network. Furthermore, Amazon also provides various analytical utilities to its FBA sellers such as reports on sales, inventory, customer concessions, and more. In return Amazon charges a fee to the seller for providing these services.

Why are FBA and Prime So Powerful?

Let's look at several hypothetical instances of varying levels complexity where FBA (the back end) and Amazon Prime (the front end) have a powerful impact.

A simple front end example on Prime from the purchaser's perspective:

Imagine you are shopping on Amazon.com for a new pair of sunglasses. You are not particularly committed to a particular brand, but seeking a particular style and a particular price. All things equal you are much more likely to select a product that includes free two day shipping over a product that does not. Speed and simplicity offers a strong incentive in the buyer's decision.

A back end example of FBA from an entrepreneur's perspective

Consider an entrepreneur who runs her own business making a very specific style of jewelry. A showroom in her home town is only going to reach a small segment of the total possible market. Even if she lives in a large city, it's unlikely that selling her niche product in an exclusive brick and mortar store would be profitable. Furthermore as a small entrepreneur, it would be a tough sell to department or chain stores to carry her products, at least in the early stages of her business. Can e-commerce solve her dilemma for how to reach a widely dispersed, but specific audience at a low cost? She can make her own website for sales and then work towards building a following on sites such as Facebook, for example. This sort of approach is certainly much closer to a solution than operating a brick and mortar store. But now let's consider how FBA and Amazon Prime might assist in this situation. She sends portions of her various product lines to Amazon FBA and lists her jewelry on Amazon Marketplace, eligible for prime. Now instead of having to worry about generating traffic for a personal website, packaging orders, handling returns, and assembling reviews, this is all essentially automated by Amazon. Her products are now easily searchable and purchasable on the website of the #1 on-line retailer in the United States[2]. In this instance, Amazon can essentially serve as a plug and play e-commerce back end for her business.

A back end example from a retail arbitrager's perspective

Let's say for example you are shopping for a music stand. You find one at your local music store that seems sturdy and is listed as good price. You decide to check Amazon.com for music stands just to make sure you are not overpaying. You see the same music stand selling for 15 dollars more on Amazon! (This can happen sometimes.) It turns out the store is also offering a "buy one, get one half off" deal on music stands. You decide to take advantage of this promotion and price discrepancy, purchase the remainder of their stock, ship it to FBA, sell on Prime, and clear a profit.

---

[2] https://nrf.com/resources/annual-retailer-lists/top-100-retailers

These examples give a small glimpse how Amazon FBA can be a powerful and efficient platform for third-party sales. The next chapter, however, will show you how this platform can be leveraged exponentially more -- this done through private labelling.

Chapter 2 - A Bird's Eye View of Private Labeling

We have seen that both the retail arbitrager and the individual entrepreneur who has a physical product to sell can benefit from the plug and play nature of Amazon's storefront and back end fulfillment process (FBA). "Great," you might say, "but I have no physical product to sell." That is perfectly fine -- private labelling is not about physically creating product -- it's about finding gaps in the market where quality generic (non-branded) products can be bought directly from suppliers and sold directly on Amazon's Marketplace at price that provides both savings to the customer and profit to you, the seller. Strategies for finding these gaps in the market will be discussed in Chapter 3. Meanwhile, the goal of this chapter is to provide a bird's eye view of the essential points of a hypothetical chain of events that create a successful private label product line on Amazon. After reading this overview, you will then understand where each of the concepts described in subsequent chapters fits into the bigger picture.

Inspiration for potential products can come from anywhere. Let's say you visiting a friend's house for a party and the lawn chair you are sitting in is unusually stylish and comfortable. You ask you friend where she obtained it -- "from a local variety store at a reasonable price." You take note of the specs in hopes to find something similar for your own yard. In searching for a similar product on Amazon, you find a very limited selection for this exact type of chair. Furthermore, the prices are higher than what your friend paid and not sold on Prime.

Under a simple retail arbitrage model, you could just acquire the rest of the stock at the variety store near your friend's house, ship the chairs to FBA, and sell them for a markup. Let's say they sell right away and you make a profit! Your hunch on this being a great market niche proved correct. But what happens next? Where do you get more chairs? This sort of business approach is not "scalable" and will not result in large-scale passive income.

Here is where private labeling comes in. Instead of simply searching at the local variety store (who is also certainly turning a profit on the item as well), you decide to skip the middle man entirely and go directly to a supplier of lawn furniture. You could start your search on Alibaba.com, for example (more on this in Chapter 4), and browse through many of the best and most affordable lawn furniture companies worldwide. From here, let's say you end up finding several China-based manufactures that carry a style that appears identical to the chair for which you are looking. You contact both manufactures and inquire about prices and the possibility of acquiring a sample order of the chairs. After comparing the options, you select one and place a sample order.

Assuming you have set up your account as a seller on Amazon (Chapter 7) and organized your business as an LLC (Chapter 8), you are set to ship your sample order to Amazon FBA and list the item. In listing the item, there are many important considerations. First, what is the image you want for this private label? You have bought the chair direct from a manufacturer, but in naming the product for the listing you have the chance to put your own spin on the product. Perhaps you choose to give the product line the general name "Garden Views." This will appear as the "by" tagline under the specific product description on the listing. Think of this as the company name. When a customer drills down into the specific listing, your company name will appear as a hyperlink "by Garden Views" and direct them to a separate page showing all of your other listings under this company name (as you expand you will have other product listings). You choose to market this particular chair as the "Piedmont Rocker." So the listing would appear something like "Piedmont Rocker - Grey/White (Outdoor), by Garden Views."

Second, what is your strategy for obtaining product reviews and optimizing the item in Amazon search? (more on this in Chapters 5 and 7) Down the road, you might end up considering some specific networking groups or tools that assist in this process, but for now, you decide to go with the simple but effective strategy at a price you believe will sell quickly and also enlisting the help of some friends willing to try the product and write a review. Getting solid reviews is an essential step in getting your product to appear near the top of the search results.

Remember that this initial listing is a great way to test demand in the market. Let's say this hypothetical case goes well for you and the sample units sell quickly and you receive solid reviews. At this point you decide to place an order with the supplier and list the products on a full scale. (In your initial discussions with the supplier, you were able to negotiate an order size that meets the risk and capital limits of your business - more on this in

As you can see, in this scenario, Garden Views is starting to cultivate a bit of a niche in lawn furniture. Simultaneously, you are developing a relationship with a quality supplier. Garden Views is just one of many possible companies that you could use to list private label products on Amazon. While Garden Views continues to generate passive income, you are doing additional research on products and scouting out new potential markets. Perhaps, you find another opportunity in fitness, for example, where a quality product can be brought to the market at a better price or a better buying choice (Prime instead of non-prime). You could brand this product under the name "Active Pursuits." You locate quality suppliers in this market and repeat the process.

A seller hopes that their market research, initial product hypothesis, and initial sample testing are reliable enough that the listing will succeed according to expectations. However, there will always be instances where a product does not meet expectations (or loses popularity after initial success). Part of being a successful business owner in being able to grasp when it is no longer effective to have you capital tied up in a certain product versus something new that promises to be more profitable .

Side Note: Active versus Passive Income

The goal of this book is to help you develop strategies and techniques for building large scale passive income. Before we proceed getting into the specifics strategies for doing this, I would like to provide a quick explanation of active versus passive income in order to get you thinking in the correct direction as we approach the topic of FBA private labeling further.

Purely active income is showing up to a daily job and working the needed hours to get the job done. If you are not working, you are not earning money. Purely passive income would be winning the lottery (wouldn't it be nice!)

or any kind of structured payment one receives in the absence of regular work to receive that payment. More practically, long-term investment income would be passive income (especially ones with a lock up period, since the investor does not even have the right to shift his money around). Bear in mind that passive income (aside from structured payments such as lottery, pension, or SSI) requires capital to invest. Meaning you commit capital and other people are putting it to work and paying you for the privilege of using your money.

Private labeling using FBA, falls somewhere between these two categories. As you build your business through locating and selling quality products, the responsibilities dedicated to those product lines diminish. You will still need to monitor sales and inventory. (If it's selling well, order more. If not, reconsider and trying to determine why.) You may also need to tweak SEO listing parameters (Chapter 5). What this increased self-sufficiency of successful products does offer is the freeing of your time to look for additional opportunities to develop your business. This might include scouting for product opportunities, seeking the best suppliers, or optimizing Amazon search engine optimization for your products. In other words, the passive elements to this approach offer the opportunity for tremendous growth -- the platform and approach allow the potential for tremendous scale. Although an FBA private labeling business can be capable of a return on investment much higher than purely passive investing, it does require some degree of startup capital. A good way to estimate the amount of startup capital you will need is to find a product you would consider selling, and then research typical minimum order quantities (MOQ) required by suppliers (more on this in Chapter 4). However, when a private label business succeeds, existing products lines reach a point where they are "selling themselves" - permitting great scalability (adding more units and more products lines) and the potential for large-scale passive income.

Chapter 3 - Strategies for Evaluating Potential Products

Now that you have a solid idea of how the process of private labelling works from a broad perspective, let's take deeper look at some of the essential elements of this type of business. Finding the exact right types of products on which to ultimately base your private labels is the absolute lifeblood an Amazon private label business. If you were to have a great "mechanical" organization to your business (efficient SEO, streamlined reports, responsive inventory management, etc.), but select the wrong products, it would be similar to having a fancy Corvette with new tires and shiny paint but a weak engine. One undoubtedly needs tires and seat to drive a car, but once these aspects are in place, the engine is the most important factor that makes the car run well or not.

Product selection is by far the most "artful" aspect of the process and it has the most considerations. By "artful" I do not mean that this part of the process relies on intuition over numbers or observed results. I mean that unlike configuring your Amazon account, this is not a process that can be fully described in an exact "A,B,C,D…" format. Being successful in product selection requires thinking conceptually as well as finding which sort of approach suits your own strengths and tastes.

A great place to start would be looking at and evaluating the general approach taken by Will Tjernland[3], one of the most successful practitioners of private labeling through Amazon. These are not hard and fast rules, but rather examples of a great way to think about the process. Your approach will likely differ somewhat.

Will looks for three general qualities when considering a product:

1) The product is a good size

2) Has minimal electronics

---

3 http://fbaexpert.com/find-great-product-fba

3) Is not a product that people exclusively buy the brand name

His reason for favoring heavier products relates to the free two day shipping incentive of Amazon Prime. There exists even more incentive to purchase through Prime if you are buying something of a higher weight (since shipping costs would be much higher if you had to foot the bill yourself). However, since he is shipping a mass order to Amazon in one shot (the initial wholesale order from the supplier), shipping charges are relatively small on a per unit basis. Furthermore, he figures that there will generally be less competition on heavier items.

The reason for favoring products with no or little electronics is simple: fewer things that can break and therefore fewer returns and negative reviews.

Reason three is essential -- it is likely very difficult to compete in a space where people almost exclusively trust brand name products. Even if a cheaper alternative is indeed viable, there exist intangible reasons why customers will still prefer purchasing brand name products. For example, take the example of golf equipment - would creating a private label for golf equipment work? Take a moment to brainstorm "why" or "why not."

A fairly precise answer to this question would be as follows: for the most part, golf equipment would be a poor candidate for selling as a private label product, but it depends on what type of golf equipment is in question. Clubs and balls would likely not be successful as the vast majority of customers who depend on time tested brands -- almost to the point of superstition. "I've been using Titleist golf balls since age ten and never plan to change." Accessories such as golf umbrellas, towels, or tees have potential, but one would need to consider margins. If the item is too inexpensive, it may be tough to make a profit after Amazon's fulfillment fees.

Conversely, something like a door weatherstrip might make an excellent private label product. Brand-wise, it would be hard to imagine anyone caring in the least who is the maker of product. Does it insulate the house from drafts or does it not?

The most important question to ask when searching for products is "how or why would a product I list gain an advantage over or gain a share along with existing products sold?" The more competitive the market, the less likely it is to be that you will be able to add value and compete. For example, if there is a gas station on every corner in your town, it probably does not make sense to open one right in between two existing ones (unless you can somehow provide a reason to make buying gas at your store better -- perhaps an attached convenience store with better food).

There are other examples besides price, where you may be able to gain an advantage (however if you do find a way to bring a quality product to the market at a better price, you may not need other advantages). For example, maybe there is a way to bundle related products in a convenient way for buyers. Or perhaps there is a niche where few products are listed on prime. Moreover, you might find a selection of products with unclear listings, poor pictures, and low response rates to questions. Bring a product to market where you do all of these things better and provide a product of exactly equal quality could be enough to gain the upper hand in that market over time. An alternate way to think about this same concept would be to take the listing and ongoing metrics outlined in the Amazon SEO (chapter 5) and evaluate how well existing listings are satisfying these metrics and if there is room for improvement.

Product ideas can come from anywhere -- such as in our hypothetical example of selling private label lawn furniture. When considering if private labeling is the right business for you, you would be well advised to start cultivating the habit of being aware of the products you use or buy on a day to day basis, looking them up, and comparing them on Amazon. Click through the related links, categories, and subcategories to get a feel an overall feel of the various markets. Chapter 7 will outline several great

utilities that assist in the process of distilling and analyzing the staggering amount of products on Amazon to find
potential private label ideas. Sometimes an idea might
come first (like with the lawn furniture) and the tool will
be useful in drilling down on this idea. For example, once
you become interested in lawn furniture you could use
tools to run an analysis on the actual sales volume of all
similar items. In some cases, using a tool might actually
be the genesis of your idea, pulling you towards potential-
ly profitable product categories at which you might not
have foreseen looking.

Trying to understand the demand in a market is just as
important as evaluating the supply (existing competitor
listings). Demand can be estimated at several stages.
First, using tools (Chapter 7), it is possible to extract data
(timing of sales, prices, total revenue). Upfront analysis
can be an effective way to compare markets on a relative
basis. Another way to assess demand is the selling of your
sample order. However, some creative sellers (Will Tjernland in this case) are taking steps to further evaluate demand in between these two stages by selling a few units

they have not bothered to actually hold. Once the units sell, they fulfill the order from another listing or buy the unit from a wholesaler and have it shipped directly to their address. Using this technique, units are sold at a slight overall loss, but this slight loss is considered an investment in information in the market (and much cheaper than making a full order).

As with any FBA related objective outlined in this book (or elsewhere), the key is to have the hunger to learn the different alternatives available for accomplishing that objective, experiment with the ones that seem promising, and determine which techniques are most suited to your particular style. For example, a seller might be a lifelong shopper who has many years of experience buying household goods for his family. Perhaps because of his tangible experience with products he is able to find niches on Amazon by more of an intuitive method -- just knowing "what people like" and at what price it will sell. Another FBA seller might be a recent graduate who does not have much experience with products but is a wizard analyzing data and trends. Both intuitive and quantitative approaches to product selection can be successful. As with any business, experimentation and trial and error are necessary. Your own approach will be crafted over time.

Chapter 4 - Finding and Evaluating Suppliers -

Alibaba.com and Other Sources

The overarching goal in searching for suppliers is to provide the best possible suppliers. Just because you are endeavoring to bring products to the market at a lower price does not mean you have to be a "snake oil salesman." In the long run, markets are intelligent. You may be able to pass an inferior product once or twice, but as you will see in the Amazon SEO chapter, Amazon's metrics are aimed at selling the best possible products and retaining customers. Customers are happy when they find value.   Value is the right mix of price and quality. For example, you might be happier paying ten dollars to see a local university jazz combo perform versus paying 200 dollars to see someone world class. While the university combo is not the best possible quality available, it is high quality given what you paid. Meanwhile, you would pay nothing -- not even your time -- to see a beginner making painful noises come from a saxophone. Buyers are making calculations like this in the marketplace every time the search for products. Keep this in mind when you search for suppliers -- you are looking for suppliers than can provide a great mix of quality and price.

Alibaba.com is the world's largest online business-to-business trading platform for small businesses. For this reason, it is very popular amongst entrepreneurs who base their private label business upon Amazon FBA. Private labelers have a vast array of global manufacturers at their fingertips. The easiest way to familiarize yourself with the site would be to simply go to the website, change the dropdown menu from products to suppliers, and enter a type for product for which you would like to view suppliers. For example, typing "lawn furniture" yields links to profiles for 634 different suppliers of these products. It's best to consider suppliers who are gold suppliers and also offer trade assurance. The gold supplier designation entails that the vendor has a premium registration with Alibaba.com. This is good check to ensure the business is credible. Trade assurance entails guarantees on quality protection and shipment protection. Once you select a company's page you can navigate between information on the company (company profile) and product categories, where you can find specifics, including pictures, relating to the types of products the company sells.

In his article entitled, "The Five Steps for Finding and Sourcing Products to Private Label and Not Getting Scammed[4]," Scott Voelker includes a template for contacting sellers which includes inquiry on essential elements such as shipping rates, sample sizes, payment policies, and flexibility regarding branding. When contacting sellers, it's best to get right to the point and screen these factors right away. If the seller requires a MOQ of 2000 units and you were hoping to buy 200, it might be easier and more fruitful to continue your search for sellers

---

4 http://theamazingseller.com/tas-006-the-5-steps-for-finding-and-sourcing-products-to-private-label-and-not-get-scammed/

than invest time in negotiating this point. That being said, if you do end up getting to the point in discussions with a supplier where you do need to negotiate the MOQ, ChinaImportal.com points out that limiting product customization, offering to pay more, and working with smaller suppliers (who are more eager to transact business) can be effective strategies.

Alibaba.com is the largest online portal for suppliers. However, Alibaba is geared towards wholesale. It is worth mentioning that their sister site AliExpress.com is geared more towards the consumer and offers much lower minimum order quantities. AliExpress may worth taking a look at if smaller orders are your objective - for example in the initial stages of testing demand or building your business. Finally, where Alibaba.com features listings for mostly Chinese suppliers, ThomasNet is a directory for United States and Canada based suppliers.

Chapter 5 - Amazon Search Engine Optimization (SEO)

Once you have selected a quality product and supplier, it is essential to make sure that the listing for the product ranks well compared to other listings. It is important to remember that Amazon uses search engine algorithms similar to a search engine like Google. Google's algorithm is designed to provide results that most closely match the search string, whereas Amazon's search algorithm is designed to provide results based on which products Amazon believes the customer is most likely to buy. Amazon answers this question by performing continuous, behind the scenes analysis of many parameters relating to each of the listings on its website. In analyzing these parameters, Amazon determines which products a customer is most likely to buy per a given search string, and then ranks the listings to appear accordingly. Structuring your listing with these parameters in mind will help you get more traffic and more sales.

In his article entitled "How to Rank Your Products on Amazon: The Ultimate Guide[5]," founder of Startupbros.com Will Mitchell nicely groups the 23 most important Amazon search factors into three general categories: conversion rate factors, relevancy factors, and customer satisfaction and retention factors. I will present this fairly exhaustive (and useful) list in aggregate and then present some strategies for breaking it down and approaching it practically.

Conversion rate factors are the ones that Amazon has found have the greatest impact on whether a customer will choose one product version another comparable product. The most important conversion rate factors are sales rank, **customer reviews**, **answered questions**, image size and quality, price, parent-child products, time on page and bounce rate, and product listing completeness.

---

5 http://startupbros.com/rank-amazon/

Relevancy factors are the factors that Amazon uses to most accurately match the content of your search string to potential products. The most important relevancy factors are title, features, product description, brand/model number, specifications, category and subcategory, search terms, and source keyword.

Customer satisfaction and retention factors are the ones that most closely correlate to the likelihood of customers making repeat purchases. The most important customer satisfaction and retention factors are negative seller feedback, order processing speed, **in-stock rate**, perfect order percentage, order defect rate, exit rate, and packaging options.

The better you understand what factors are used and the intent behind how Amazon categorizes them (conversion, relevancy, and satisfaction), the better you will grasp why products are listed in the way they are. You will start to notice specific attributes of other successful listings and be able to incorporate them into your own. Building knowledge of each of these factors and how they relate should be an ongoing effort (if you desire more detail, please see Will's guide mentioned above).

Trying to consider all of these factors simultaneously is daunting. Fortunately, they can be broken down in a way that gets you moving in the right direction immediately:

First of all, there are many factors in Amazon's algorithm over which the seller has no direct control, but rather are the result of other factors or are controlled by the customer entirely. Sales rank, time on page and bounce rate, negative seller feedback, order defect rate, and exit rate are all controlled by customer behaviors. Order processing speed, perfect order percentage, and packaging options will be controlled by Amazon since Amazon is the one fulfilling the order (FBA). These factors are the ends we seek but not the means to those ends. So let's worry about the factors we can control.

You may have noticed that all of the factors above which are underlined are parameters of the actual listing itself. These factors constitute more than half of the 23 most important ranking factors! The most important takeaway from this chapter is spend time creating your listing and be observant of other listings in order to incorporate successful practices into your own listings. Put emphasis on carefully crafting your listing and you will achieve better SEO results. Some examples of effective listing practices are as follows:

•Use several high quality, higher resolution photographs which completely show the product.

•Group variations of your product (size, color, etc.) under the same listing as opposed to creating several listings.

•Make the title as descriptive as possible without becoming unwieldy. Include brand name and mode number in the title.

•Clearly list all product features.

•Create a well written product description that expands upon the product features in a succinct manner. Highlight notable distinctions.

•Include an accurate and organized list of relevant technical specifications.

•Place product in most appropriate product category.

•Brainstorm or research relevant search terms to pair with listing.

The items listed in **bold** (answered questions and in-stock rate) are ongoing matters. Promptly answering all customer questions will positively contribute to your product ranking. Likewise, you will boost your ranking by not running out of stock where there is demand for the product. Monitor the inventory of your products and plan the timing of order from suppliers (and shipping to FBA) accordingly to avoid unwanted stock-outs.

Finally, customer reviews are an essential element of Amazon SEO over which you have some degree of control. This can also be considered an ongoing matter, but it deserves its own mention as there are various strategies for optimizing your listing that revolve around customer reviews. Consider the following scenario: you have a solid product that you are bringing to market -- you have found and excellent supplier and you have taken all the right steps to create a listing. However, at this point you lack product reviews. At this point, reviews are the catalyst that will get your product selling. Often the best strategy from here is to either give away several units (or sell at a discount depending on initial price) in exchange for reviews. There are plenty of websites and groups discussed in Chapter 6 that can assist in pairing you with people will to review your products.

Chapter 6 – Tools and Utilities

This chapter outlines some tools and utilities that may be helpful to your private labeling business. Tools are designed to assist in accomplishing objectives outlined in the prior chapters. Please do not be intimidated by the amount of products that exist to help FBA business owners, but no means it is necessary to use all (or even most) of these products. I would suggest you experiment with adding them into your workflow as needed. For example, if you find the amount of data you are churning through while searching for products to be overwhelming, there are tools that help extract, aggregate, and organize this relevant data into an organized manner. Similarly there are a vast number of tools designed to assist with, automate, and enhance many element of the Amazon SEO process. Experiment and see what works for you. It is also worth bearing in mind that a lot of these tools increase in value along with the scale of your business. This is especially true with inventory and tax related products. As you build your business it may be the easiest and most cost effective to simply tackle many of those processes manually with Excel. As your business grows, the value you realize by incorporating automation increases (relative to the fixed price you pay for the service).

The below list was compiled by Scott Voelker of TheAmazingSeller.com[6]. I include a brief description of each tool and how it might help, but please visit the respective websites for more information.

Product Research (assist with goals outlined in Chapter 4)

Jungle Scout - junglescout.com

Jungle Scout offers a chrome extension and a web app, each with various   features aimed at greatly reducing time spent searching for potential products. Their products grab data from Amazon.com and present it in a way to help you make informed decisions based on data rather than intuition.

---

[6] http://theamazingseller.com/top-resources-for-fba-private-label-sellers/

CamelCamelCamel - camelcamelcamel.com

This is a free price tracker that allows you to enter selections of products or types of products and monitor their fluctuations as opposed to having to click through a bunch of listings. This site can be good for scouting out various sectors or monitoring competition.

Google Trends - google.com/trends

Google trends does what the name sounds like --tracks trends for the web searches on its site. For example, if you type "hats", you will see that interest in this product peaks exactly in December of each year -- no surprise there! Can be useful tool to estimate whether there is growing or declining demand in a given product segment.

Amasuite 4 - getamasuite.com

AmaSuite is a software based tool designed for extracting and compiling data from Amazon. For example, it can extract all of the top 100 lists across the major product categories in one shot. This product can also assist with keyword tracking a product reviews.

Finding Suppliers (Chapter 5)

Alibaba - alibaba.com

World's largest online business-to-business trading platform for small businesses. Great for finding suppliers internationally.

AliExpress - aliexpress.com

Products listed by international (mostly Chinese) suppliers. Minimum order quantities on AliExpess can be as low as one item whereas Alibaba is geared towards wholesale.

ThomasNet - thomasnet.com

Platform for searching suppliers based out of the United States and Canada.

Amazon SEO (Chapter 6)

Product Reviews

GetBSR - getbsr.com

This is essentially a group of buyers that specialize in delivering reviews. You can provide a one-time coupon for them to purchase the product and they will write a review. The group maintains high ethical standards, so you will need to ship them a great product to great a great review. They take measures not to over-click your listing and hurt your conversion rate.

Tomoson - tomoson.com   **Viral Launch** - viral-launch.com **Snag-Shout** - snagshout.com

These sites allow to you to connect with bloggers or other online reviewers who will test and review your product in order to generate positive review momentum. Each site has a slight different spin and approach. Viral Launch also offers several other listing optimization services.

Keyword Research and Tracking

Google Keyword Planner - adword.google.com/keywordplanner

Google Keyword Planner allows you to search for keyword ideas, get historical statistics, see how keywords might perform, and test sample strings. This tool is very useful in helping create the keywords to be attached to your Amazon listing.

Merchant Words - merchantwords.com

Merchant Words has collected over 40 million of the most searched terms on Amazon. They also break down the search terms by category which as be useful in assigning categories.

Keyword Inspector - keywordinspector.com

Keyword Inspector has aggregated a massive database of searches and product keywords. You can also search keywords, products, and trends by average price, review count, sales rank, sales per day, and rating.

AMZ Shark - amzshark.com

AMZ Shark allows you to spy on the actual sales volume for any product, split test your listing pages, and compare competitors keywords against your own.

Legal, Accounting, and Tax (Chapter 8)

LegalZoom - legalzoom.com

Affordable, readily available legal advice for all matters. Could be useful for setting up your LLC or trademarks.

CPA on Fire - cpaonfire.com

Accounting tips, resources, and services geared towards entrepreneurs. As your business picks up steam, you will be in a much better position if you tackle tax and accounting setup matters as early as possible as opposed to unraveling it retroactively.

Waves - waveapps.com

Waves is a free cloud based accounting application.

Freshbooks - freshbooks.com

Another cloud based accounting application. Freshbooks is more comprehensive than waves, but requires a subscription.

Stitch Labs - stitchlabs.com

Stitch labs inventory management software can greatly automate your inventory control process. It also offers variations integration and reporting features.

TaxJar - taxjar.com

TaxJar automates the process of sales tax reporting.

Ongoing Business Matters, Miscellaneous

Brand Builders - brandbuilders.io

Brand Builders focuses on website design and related branding. As your business grows, working with specialized professionals in this area could add credibility to your brand.

Listing Eagle - listingeagle.com

Security services that prevent your listing from getting hijacked. This service would be worth listing in if security becomes an issue with your listings.

Elemerce - elemerce.com

A business consulting group that has deep expertise in Amazon private labeling. Working with these consultants could be a viable option as your business starts to grow to a large size.

Sales Backer - salesbacker.com   **Feedback Genious** - sellerlabs.com

AWeber - aweber.com   **Leadpages** - leadpages.net

The above services focus on the automation and organization of email and feedback.

Chapter 7 – Great Resources for Further Reading

Amazon.com

Your most essential resource for all the technical and logistical elements relating to the Fulfillment By Amazon element of your business will be the Help section on Amazon's website. There is an entire section related to FBA including an introduction to the service and detailed sections on policies and requirements, features and fees, managing FBA inventory, and FBA business analytics. The best place to start would be the 26-page quick start guide that they offer. It covers topics such as creating an FBA account, product labeling (UPC, Amazon product labels, stickerless, etc.), product packaging, shipping requirements, inventory placement, prepping products, and more.

TheAmazingSeller.com

This is Scott Voelker's website devoted to all topics FBA. There are hundreds of pointed articles, tutorials, discussions, anecdotes, and podcasts on this site that cover pretty much every element of the private labeling process.

HonestFew.com

Honest Few is an online community for reviewing products on Amazon. There is a useful section called "FBA University" that contains a wealth of knowledge.

StartupBros.com

StartupBros is a comprehensive website started by Will Mitchell and Kyle Eschenroeder. There is a forum specifically related to importing and e-commerce. Here, you can find discussions and articles covering topics such as product research, dealing with suppliers, shipping and freight, fulfillment, and more.

FBAexpert.com

This is the blog operated by Will Tjernland, who is one of the most successful practitioners of private labeling using Amazon FBA. His articles are short and to-the-point, but absolutely packed with content. There are many tech heavy resources on the web, but Will's articles go beyond mechanics and discuss core strategies for building the business. He offers and candid view of the future of FBA and does not sugar coat things. Topics include tips for using Alibaba.com, attending trade fairs, Amazon SEO, product selection, and more.

<u>Amazon Advantage: Product Listing Strategies to Boost Your Sales</u>

This book by Karon Thackston is an excellent guide for assembling better Amazon Listings (Chapter 5). She offers many strategies for tapping into the mindset behind Amazon's metrics and making your listings stand out.

Chapter 8 – Importance of Legal Structure

I would like to note up front that no advice in this section should be considered to be legal or tax advice. Please consult a CPA or attorney for definitive counsel on tax or legal matters.

That said, the purpose of this section is to highlight some of the benefits and considerations involved in creating the right legal structure for your Amazon private labelling business. It is important to remember that in selling products to the general public, it might be possible for you, the business owner, to incur liability if something were to go wrong with one of your products. If you are simply running the business under your own name and a claim was made against you, your personal assets could be at stake. Similarly, if your business incurred debt, your personal assets could also be subject to a claim.

Organizing your private labelling business as an LLC will protect your personal assets and credit against these eventualities. In addition protecting your personal assets and credit from business related claims, organizing as an LLC also can yield tax advantages, increased credibility, and flexibility in ownership structure in the event you wish to add a partner to the business.

Conclusion

Sellers are scouring Amazon each day looking for opportunities to enhance their listings or bring new products to market. Like any competitive market, sellers, by competing against each other to win over buyers in turn make the market more efficient - more products are offered at better prices. Despite the fact that Amazon.com has become increasingly competitive for third-party sellers, opportunities to earn large-scale passive income still exist for those driven and creative enough to find them.

Perhaps you are interested in some of the concepts outlined in the book and wish to take steps towards creating a business. If so, I would advocate making some "dry runs" through Amazon and a supplier portal such as Alibaba. Although many tools and utilities are available, I would not get bogged down with these products in the early stages of experimenting with the concepts that drive FBA business. First, determine whether you are fascinated and inspired by the idea of learning Amazon and searching for and evaluating products. Simply click around as deeply as you can go into the various listings on the site and make broad assessments of factors such as competition, price, and quality of the listings. Start thinking about the products you use and buy each day and how they may or may not be effectively sold on Amazon. When one pops into your head, look it up on Amazon and perform the same sort of assessment. Trace these products all the way back to the supplier if you can. Familiarizing yourself in this sort of manner should give you a great idea of whether or not this business is right for you.

Do solid due diligence. Do consider the viability of your venture and if you will enjoy this type of work. Do take your time in assessing whether you can add value in market segments. Do take time becoming very familiar with the variety of tools available to assist in the process. Do consider legal and tax issues ahead of time. But when you have done these things, DO NOT be afraid of failure. Part of being a successful a successful entrepreneur is the ability to go out on a limb and take calculated risks without knowing what the exact results will be. Many of history's greatest figures in the area of commerce failed numerous times before breaking through. Be flexible and resilient.

When the time comes to take the plunge and make your first order, go for it! You will be ready. Start the journey.

Finally, if you enjoyed this book, then I'd like to ask you for a favor, would you be kind enough to leave a review for this book on Amazon? It would be greatly appreciated! It helps me rank on amazon.

Go to amazon to leave a review for this book on Amazon!

Thank you and good luck!

Ps. Don't miss you free bonus on the next page given by one of my friends.

FREE Bonus!

Want To Make a Passive Income While You Lay On The Beach Somewhere?

Or whatever you like to do instead of working….

Passive Income Blueprint.

Visit www.GreenSleeper.com to get free tips about how you can make serious money while doing anything else! Sleeping, laying on the beach, traveling, only your imagination is the limit! The guy who has the site makes his money from kindle. However, he does not even write the books himself!? Yes it is true. And still he is able to generate thousands of dollars of income!

At the moment you can get a FREE download of:

The "Make Money While You Sleep" Guide

But hurry up, the guide will not be there forever!

Visit My Friends Website And Download It Now! 100% Free! What Do You Have To Lose?

If you don't want the guide, read the blog which can teach you a lot of things about the kindle business, business mindset and much much more!